The Art of Writing

A
Bestselling Textbook

Stefano
Garner

To God, Mom, & Dad

CONTENTS

INTRODUCTION

Welcome to the world of educational publishing! Writing a bestselling textbook can be an incredibly rewarding and impactful endeavor. This book is designed to equip you with the essential knowledge and strategies to create a textbook that resonates with readers, educators, and students alike. Whether you are an experienced educator or a subject matter expert looking to share your knowledge, this book will walk you through the entire process of crafting a successful textbook that stands out in the market.

TARGET AUDIENCE

Before you embark on the journey of writing a bestselling textbook, it is crucial to understand who your target audience is. Your audience will play a pivotal role in shaping the content, style, and overall success of your textbook. In this chapter, we will explore the process of identifying your readership, understanding their needs and pain points, and conducting market research to ensure your textbook meets the demands of the educational landscape.

Identifying Your Target Readership

The first step in writing a bestselling textbook is to define who you are writing for. Are you targeting students, educators, or both? Each group has distinct requirements, and tailoring your content to their specific needs is essential for creating a valuable resource.

Students

If your primary audience is students, consider their academic level, age range, and educational background. Are you writing for high school students, undergraduate learners, or graduate students?

Understanding their existing knowledge and learning preferences, will help you present information in a way that resonates with them.

Educators

If educators are your primary audience, identify the subjects they teach and the level of expertise they possess. Are you writing for K-12 teachers, college professors, or vocational instructors? Recognizing their goals and challenges will enable you to address their instructional needs effectively.

Some textbooks cater to both students and educators simultaneously. In such cases, strike a balance between academic rigor and pedagogical support. This dual approach can create a comprehensive learning experience for both parties.

Once you have identified your target audience, delve deeper into their needs and pain points.

Ask yourself the following questions

What Learning Goals Do They Have?
Understand the learning objectives your audience aims to achieve through your textbook.

Are they seeking foundational knowledge, advanced skills, or problem-solving techniques?
Tailoring your content to meet these objectives will ensure its relevance and value.

What Are Their Challenges?
Identify the common struggles and obstacles your audience faces in the subject matter. Addressing these challenges directly will make your textbook indispensable, as readers will find solutions to their difficulties.

How Can Your Textbook Help?
Clearly articulate how your textbook can address the needs and challenges of your audience. Highlight its unique selling proposition (USP) and explain how it stands out from existing resources.

Market Research

Conducting thorough market research is vital for understanding the competitive landscape and identifying gaps in existing educational materials. Here are some steps to guide your research.

Evaluate Competing Textbooks

Analyze textbooks that cover similar topics and compare their strengths and weaknesses. This analysis will help you identify areas where your textbook can offer a fresh perspective or improved content.

Gather Feedback from Educators and Students

Seek input from educators and students in the relevant field through surveys, focus groups, or interviews. Their insights can provide valuable guidance in tailoring your content to meet their expectations.

Consider Technological Advances

Explore the integration of technology in educational materials. Digital resources, interactive platforms, and online learning tools are becoming increasingly popular. Assess how your textbook can leverage these advances to enhance the learning experience.

Summary

Understanding your target audience is the foundation of writing a bestselling textbook. By identifying your readership, empathizing with their needs, and conducting thorough market research, you will be equipped to create a textbook that resonates with your audience and makes a lasting impact in the educational landscape. keep your audience at the forefront throughout the writing process, and you will lay the groundwork for a successful and influential textbook.

UNIQUE
SELLING
PROPOSITION

In the competitive world of educational publishing, having a clear and compelling Unique Selling Proposition (USP) is essential for writing a bestselling textbook. Your USP is what sets your book apart from others in the market and communicates its unique value to your target audience. In this chapter, we will explore the process of defining your USP, understanding the distinctive qualities of your textbook, and crafting a vision that captivates both educators and students.

The Power of Your Textbook's Uniqueness

Before you can define your USP, take a moment to reflect on what makes your textbook different.

Consider the following aspects:

Subject Matter Expertise

What expertise and qualifications do you bring to the subject matter? Highlighting your credentials as an author or the expertise of your team can instill confidence in readers that they are learning1 from a credible source.

Innovative Approach

Does your textbook present the material in a fresh and innovative way? Whether it's through engaging storytelling, interactive elements, or problem-solving exercises, innovation can make your textbook stand out.

Unexplored Topics or Perspectives

Does your book cover topics that are often overlooked or provide unique perspectives on familiar subjects? Offering new insights can attract readers seeking a deeper understanding of the subject.

Pedagogical Support

Does your textbook go beyond conveying information to actively supporting the learning process? Clear explanations, well-structured lessons, and practical examples can enhance the educational experience. and most successful books either address all of the above points or at least some of them.

Compelling Vision

Your USP should be aligned with a captivating vision for your textbook.

Think about the impact you want it to have on your readers and the educational community as a whole.

Setting Clear Goals

Define the primary goals of your textbook. Is it to make learning more accessible, to inspire a love for the subject, or to equip students with practical skills for real-world application? Having clear goals will guide your writing and resonate with your audience.

Addressing the Audience's Needs

Revisit the needs and pain points of your target audience, as discussed in Chapter 1. Your vision should directly address how your textbook will fulfil those needs and provide valuable solutions.

Creating a Brand Persona

Just like any successful product, your textbook can have a "brand persona." Consider the tone, style, and personality you want your book to convey. A strong brand persona helps create a memorable and relatable experience for readers.

Communicating Your USP Effectively

Once you have defined your USP and crafted a captivating vision, it's crucial to communicate them effectively to your audience.

Clear and Concise Messaging

Express your USP and vision in clear and concise language. Avoid jargon and technical terms that may alienate readers. Your messaging should be easily understood by educators, students, and anyone interested in your subject matter.

Use of Marketing Materials

Leverage various marketing materials to convey your USP. These may include book cover design, promotional videos, website content, and social media posts. Consistency in messaging across all platforms is key.

Engaging with Your Audience

Interact with your potential readers through social media, blog posts, or webinars. Engage in conversations to understand their expectations and tailor your USP to better meet their needs.

Summary

Defining your Unique Selling Proposition (USP) and creating a captivating vision for your textbook are crucial steps in writing a bestselling educational resource. By understanding the distinctiveness of your book, aligning it with clear goals and audience needs, and effectively communicating its value, you will be well-positioned to capture the attention of educators and students alike. Embrace your book's uniqueness and let it shine as you move forward in the writing process

PLANNING

Now that you have a clear understanding of your target audience and a well-defined Unique Selling Proposition (USP), it's time to embark on the planning and outlining phase of writing your bestselling textbook. This chapter will guide you through the process of structuring your textbook, designing chapters and sections, and writing learning objectives that align with your vision and the needs of your audience.

Structuring Your Textbook

Creating a well-organized and coherent structure is essential for a successful textbook. The structure should guide smoothly through the material and facilitate their learning journey.

Define the Overall Framework

Start by outlining the major sections or units of your textbook. These units should follow a logical progression and cover the essential topics related to your subject matter.

Chapter Breakdown

Within each unit, plan the individual chapters Break down the content into manageable segments that cover specific themes or concepts. Ensure that each chapter builds upon the previous ones and contributes to the overall learning objectives.

Flow and Transition

Pay attention to the flow and transition between chapters. Smoothly guide readers from one topic to another, avoiding abrupt changes or disconnection between sections. This might happen when you are collaborating with one or more authors

Designing Chapters and Sections

Now that you have an overall structure, it's time to design the chapters and sections in detail. This step will give you a clear roadmap for writing each part of your textbook.

Introduction and Overview

Begin each chapter with a compelling introduction that sets the stage for what readers will learn. Provide an overview of the chapter's content to give them a sense of direction.

Subheadings and Subsections

Organize the content within each chapter using subheadings and subsections. These headings should be descriptive and highlight the key points covered in each section.

Incorporating Examples and Case Studies

Consider including relevant examples, case studies, or real-life scenarios to illustrate concepts and engage readers. Practical applications of the material can enhance the learning experience.

Exercises and Practice Questions

Integrate exercises and practice questions throughout the chapters. These interactive elements encourage active learning and help readers reinforce their understanding.

Writing Learning Objectives

Learning objectives are crucial for guiding your writing and ensuring that your textbook meets the needs of your audience. Learning objectives clearly state what readers should be able to achieve after studying each chapter.

Be Specific and Measurable

Ensure that your learning objectives are specific and measurable. Avoid vague statements and focus on clear, observable outcomes.

Align with Bloom's Taxonomy

Consider using Bloom's Taxonomy to categorize your learning objectives based on cognitive levels, such as remembering, understanding, applying, analyzing, evaluating, and creating.

Connect to Overall Goals

Keep the overall goals of your textbook in mind when writing learning objectives. Each objective should contribute to fulfilling the vision you outlined in Chapter 2.

Summary

Planning and outlining your textbook lays the groundwork for a well-structured and impactful educational resource. By carefully designing the structure, chapters, and sections, and writing clear learning objectives, you create a roadmap that aligns with your vision and meets the needs of your target audience. The planning phase sets the stage for the actual writing process, empowering you to create a coherent, engaging, and effective textbook that resonates with educators and students alike. As you move forward, remember to stay true to your Unique Selling Proposition and keep the needs of your readers at the forefront of your work.

ENGAGING
CONTENT

Now that you have a well-planned outline and clear learning objectives for your textbook, it's time to focus on the heart of your book: the content. Writing engaging content is essential for capturing and retaining the attention of your readers, making the learning experience enjoyable and impactful. In this chapter, we will explore various strategies and techniques to create content that not only educates but also inspires, informs, and captivates your target audience.

Understanding the Power of Storytelling

One of the most effective ways to engage readers is through storytelling. Human beings are naturally drawn to narratives, and integrating stories into your textbook can make complex concepts more relatable and memorable.

Use Real-Life Examples

Incorporate real-life examples and anecdotes that demonstrate the practical application of the subject matter. Personal stories or case studies can provide context and relevance, making the content more meaningful to your audience.

Present Historical Context

If applicable to your subject, provide historical context or narratives of influential figures related to the topic. This historical perspective can enrich the readers' understanding and appreciation of the subject's development.

Connect Concepts through Narratives

Create narratives that thread through the chapters, connecting different concepts and demonstrating their interconnectedness. This continuity can enhance comprehension and retention of the material.

Crafting Clear and Concise Prose

Clarity and conciseness are paramount in educational writing. Readers should be able to understand complex ideas without getting bogged down in convoluted language.

Avoid Jargon and Technical Language

Minimize the use of jargon and technical terms, especially without proper explanations. Instead, use straightforward language that makes the content accessible to readers of all backgrounds.

Break Down Complex Concepts

When presenting intricate ideas, break them down into digestible chunks. Use analogies or metaphors to illustrate complex concepts in familiar terms.

Be Succinct yet Comprehensive

Strive for brevity without sacrificing important details. Focus on delivering information efficiently, ensuring that each sentence contributes to the overall understanding of the topic.

Utilizing Multimedia and Visuals

Integrating multimedia and visuals can significantly enhance the engagement and comprehension of your textbook.

Incorporate Illustrations and Graphics

Use relevant illustrations, charts, graphs, and diagrams to visually represent data and concepts. Visual aids can simplify complex information and reinforce key points.

Include High-Quality Images

If appropriate, include high-quality images that support the content and add visual appeal to your textbook.

Interactive Elements

Consider incorporating interactive elements, such as QR codes, augmented reality (AR), or online resources. these features can offer additional context or supplementary material.

Encouraging Active Learning

Promote active learning throughout your textbook to keep readers engaged and deepen their understanding.

Thought-Provoking Questions

Pose thought-provoking questions or prompts to encourage readers to reflect on the material. This fosters critical thinking and self-assessment.

Interactive Exercises and Activities

Integrate interactive exercises, activities, and quizzes that encourage readers to apply the knowledge they've gained.

Provide Opportunities for Reflection

Incorporate space for readers to jot down notes, ideas, or reflections on the material. This helps reinforce learning and personalizes the reading experience.

Summary

Writing engaging content is a crucial aspect of crafting a bestselling textbook. By incorporating storytelling, maintaining clarity in prose, utilizing multimedia, and encouraging active learning, you can create a dynamic and immersive learning experience for your readers. Engaging content not only captures attention but also leaves a lasting impact on the minds of educators and students, making your textbook a valuable resource in the educational landscape. As you progress in your writing journey, stay true to your vision, and continue to prioritize the needs and interests of your target audience.

COLLABORATION

Writing a bestselling textbook is often a collaborative effort that involves expertise from multiple individuals. Collaboration and peer review are essential components of the writing process that ensure the quality, accuracy, and comprehensiveness of your educational resource. In this chapter, we will explore the benefits of collaboration, how to effectively work with co-authors and subject matter experts, and the importance of peer review in refining your textbook.

The Value of Collaboration

Collaboration brings diverse perspectives and expertise to the table, enriching the content and overall quality of your textbook.

Assembling a Collaborative Team

Identify potential co-authors or contributors who possess expertise in complementary areas. A collaborative team can pool together different insights and knowledge, resulting in a well-rounded and comprehensive textbook.

Delegating Responsibilities

Clearly define roles and responsibilities within the collaborative team. Assign specific chapters or sections to each team member based on their expertise and interests.

Maintaining Communication

Effective communication is the foundation of successful collaboration. Establish regular meetings or communication channels to discuss progress, exchange ideas, and address any challenges that arise.

Co-Authors and Subject Matter Experts

Collaborating with co-authors and subject matter experts can significantly enhance the credibility and authority of your textbook.

Respecting Individual Contributions

Acknowledge and respect the expertise of each co-author or contributor. Embrace diverse viewpoints and work together to integrate different perspectives seamlessly.

Reviewing and Consolidating Content

Regularly review the content produced by co-authors and subject matter experts. Ensure that the material aligns with the overall vision and learning objectives of the textbook.

Maintaining Consistency

Strive for consistency in writing style, terminology, and formatting across the entire textbook. A cohesive presentation enhances the overall reading experience.

The Importance of Peer Review

Peer review is a critical step in the writing process that involves seeking feedback from impartial reviewers.

Selecting Reviewers

Choose reviewers who are experts in the subject matter and possess a keen eye for detail. Their objective feedback can identify areas of improvement and potential errors.

Reviewing for Accuracy and Clarity

Ask reviewers to assess the accuracy of the content and the clarity of explanations. Are the concepts well-presented and easy to understand?

Gathering Constructive Feedback

Encourage reviewers to provide constructive feedback that identifies strengths and weaknesses in the textbook. Use this feedback to refine and enhance the content.

Addressing Reviewer Feedback

Thoroughly evaluate and incorporate reviewer feedback into your revisions. Address any concerns or suggestions raised by the reviewers to improve the overall quality of the textbook.

Summary

Collaboration and peer review play pivotal roles in the creation of a bestselling textbook. Working with a collaborative team of co-authors and subject matter experts enriches the content with diverse perspectives and expertise. Additionally, peer review provides valuable external feedback that ensures accuracy and clarity.

Embrace the collaborative process and value the insights of your peers and reviewers, as they will help you refine and elevate your textbook to its full potential. By engaging in open communication, fostering a spirit of mutual respect, and embracing constructive criticism, you can create an educational resource that resonates with educators and students, making a lasting impact on the field of education.

THE
APPEARANCE

The cover page, title, and subtitle of your textbook serve as the first impression for potential readers. A well-designed cover and carefully chosen title can capture attention, convey the essence of your educational resource, and contribute to its overall success. In this chapter, we will delve into the art of creating an appealing cover page, selecting a compelling title, and crafting a subtitle that succinctly communicates the essence of your bestselling textbook.

The Power of a Visual Cover

The cover page is the face of your textbook and plays a crucial role in attracting readers.

Visual Elements

Consider incorporating relevant images, illustrations, or graphics that represent the subject matter of your textbook. Visuals should resonate with your target audience and convey the book's theme.

Typography

Choose fonts that reflect the tone of your textbook whether it's formal, approachable, or innovative. Ensure readability, even in thumbnail sizes, to captivate potential readers.

Color Palette

Select a color scheme that evokes the mood and theme of your textbook. Colors can influence emotions and perceptions, so choose hues that align with your content.

Crafting an Intriguing Title

The title of your textbook is a significant component of its identity and should pique the curiosity of potential readers.

Reflect the Content

Choose a title that provides insight into the core content of your textbook. It should give readers a sense of what to expect and align with the subject matter.

Be Clear and Concise

A concise title is memorable and easier for readers to remember and share. Avoid overly complex or ambiguous titles that might confuse potential readers.

Captivate with Creativity

Inject creativity and originality into your title to make it stand out among other educational resources. A clever or unique title can generate interest and curiosity.

Crafting an Informative Subtitle

The subtitle complements the title by providing additional context and clarifying the focus of your textbook.

Define the Scope

Use the subtitle to define the scope or intended audience of your textbook. Specify the educational level, subject area, or target demographic to provide clarity.

Highlight Unique Selling Points

If your textbook offers distinct advantages or features, highlight them in the subtitle. This can attract readers looking for specific benefits.

Convey Benefits

Explain the benefits that readers can gain from using your textbook. Whether it's improved skills, comprehensive knowledge, or practical applications, the subtitle should communicate value.

Iterative Design and Testing

Creating an appealing cover page, title, and subtitle is an iterative process that requires testing and refinement.

Gather Feedback

Share potential cover designs, titles, and subtitles with a diverse group of individuals, including peers, educators, and potential readers. Use their feedback to make informed decisions.

Consider Market Trends

Research current design and titling trends in the educational publishing industry. While staying unique is important, aligning with trends can make your textbook more appealing to your target audience.

Test Across Formats

Ensure that your cover design, title, and subtitle are visually appealing and legible in various formats, including print and digital thumbnails.

Summary

Crafting an appealing cover page, title, and subtitle requires careful consideration of visual design, messaging, and audience appeal. A well-designed cover can draw readers in, while a compelling title and informative subtitle provide context and generate interest. Embrace the iterative process of design and testing to create a cover page that effectively represents the essence of your educational resource. By investing time and creativity into this crucial aspect of your textbook, you enhance its marketability and increase the likelihood of capturing the attention of educators and students, ultimately contributing to the success of your bestselling textbook.

NAVIGATING PUBLISHING INDUSTRY

Navigating the publishing industry is a crucial aspect of bringing your bestselling textbook to life. Understanding the different publishing options, choosing the right approach, and successfully engaging with publishers are essential steps in the publication process. In this chapter, we will explore the pros and cons of traditional publishing versus self-publishing, how to find the right publisher for your textbook, and important considerations when negotiating contracts and royalties.

Traditional Publishing vs. Self-Publishing

Before deciding on a publishing route, it's essential to weigh the advantages and disadvantages of both traditional publishing and self-publishing.

Traditional Publishing

Pros:
Established Distribution Channels: Traditional publishers have wide-ranging distribution networks, enabling your textbook to reach a broad audience.

Editorial and Design Support: Professional editing, proofreading, and book design services are typically provided by traditional publishers.

Credibility and Recognition: Being published by a reputable publishing house lends credibility to your textbook and can enhance its recognition.

Cons:
Lengthy Publishing Process: Traditional publishing may involve a more extended period from manuscript submission to book release.
Less Control Over Content: Publishers may have input into content changes and decisions.
Royalties and Advances: Authors may receive a lower percentage of royalties and may need to negotiate advance payments.

Self-Publishing

Pros:
Greater Control: Authors have full control over the content, design, and release timeline of their textbook.

Higher Royalties: Self-published authors often retain a larger percentage of book sales as royalties.

Faster Publication: The self-publishing process allows for quicker release of the textbook.

Cons:

Marketing and Distribution: Self-published authors are responsible for marketing and distribution, which may require additional efforts and expenses.

Quality Control: Without the support of traditional publishing resources, authors need to ensure professional editing and design.

I would recommend that you go for the best of both worlds by first self-publishing (you can control the digital version sales and Royalties) and then choosing the right publishers only for the print version (so you get the best possible distribution channel, additional marketing support, and piracy control in the case the title becomes a bestseller).

Finding the Right Publisher

If you choose the traditional publishing route, finding the right publisher is crucial for the success of your textbook.

Researching Publishers

Identify publishers specializing in your subject area or educational level. Research their previous publications, reputation, and market reach.

Book Proposal

Prepare book proposals that succinctly introduce your textbook and outline its unique selling points. Tailor your submissions to each publisher to demonstrate your understanding of their audience and market.

Building Relationships

Establish connections with publishers through conferences, workshops, and networking events. Personal relationships can enhance your chances of getting noticed and published.

Understanding Contracts and Royalties

Negotiating a publishing contract is a crucial step in protecting your rights and ensuring fair compensation for your work.

Legal Review

Seek legal advice or representation to review the terms of the publishing contract. Ensure that you understand all clauses, rights granted, and obligations as an author.

Royalties and Advances

Negotiate royalty rates and any potential advances. Be aware of industry standards and advocate for fair compensation for your contributions.

Rights and Permissions

Understand the rights you are granting to the publisher, including copyright ownership, translation rights, and electronic rights.

Marketing and Promotion

Discuss the publisher's marketing and promotional plans for your textbook. Collaborate on strategies to ensure your book reaches the intended audience effectively.

Summary

Navigating the publishing industry requires careful consideration of the pros and cons of traditional publishing versus self-publishing. Finding the right publisher involves researching and building relationships within the industry. When negotiating contracts and royalties, prioritize your rights as an author and advocate for fair compensation. Whichever path you choose, remember that successful publishing is not solely about the publication itself but also about effectively reaching your target audience. Embrace the opportunities and challenges of the publishing process, and your hard work and dedication will lead to a well-received and influential bestselling textbook.

MARKETING
AND
PROMOTION

"The Author is the Star of the Book."

Writing a bestselling textbook is just the beginning of your journey. To ensure the success of your educational resource, effective marketing and promotion are essential. In this chapter, we will explore the importance of a well-crafted marketing plan, leveraging digital platforms, engaging with your audience, and building a community around your textbook.

Creating a Marketing Plan

A comprehensive marketing plan is the backbone of successful textbook promotion. It outlines your promotional strategies, target audience, and distribution channels.

Identifying Your Target Market

Define your primary target market—educators, students, or both—and understand their preferences, interests, and needs. Tailoring your marketing efforts to your audience ensures better engagement.

Setting Clear Objectives

Establish specific marketing objectives, such as increasing book sales, expanding market reach, or fostering a community of educators using your textbook.

Choosing Promotion Channels

Select a mix of promotional channels, including online platforms, educational conferences, workshops, and partnerships with educational institutions.

Budgeting and Scheduling

Allocate a budget for marketing activities and create a schedule that optimizes your promotional efforts over time.

Leveraging Digital Platforms

In the digital age, online platforms are invaluable for reaching a global audience and building brand awareness.

Website and Blog

Create a dedicated website for your textbook, providing information about the book, author, and supporting resources. A blog can be used to share updates, insights, and educational content related to your subject matter.

Social Media Marketing

Harness the power of social media to connect with educators, students, and other stakeholders. Engage with your audience through platforms like Twitter, Facebook, LinkedIn, and Instagram.

Email Marketing

Build an email list of interested educators and students. Use email newsletters to share valuable content, updates, and exclusive offers related to your textbook.

Online Advertising

Consider using targeted online advertising to reach your specific audience segments.

Engaging with Your Audience

Interacting with your audience fosters a sense of community and encourages brand loyalty.

Respond to Feedback

Encourage readers to provide feedback and respond to comments, questions, and concerns promptly.

Conduct Webinars and Workshops

Organize webinars and workshops related to your textbook's subject matter. These events can demonstrate the value of your educational resource and deepen engagement with your audience.

Offer Support and Resources

Provide additional resources, such as supplementary materials, study guides, and practice questions, to support educators and students using your textbook.

A Community around Your Textbook

Establishing a community of educators and learners fosters a loyal user base and encourages word-of-mouth marketing.

Online Forums and Groups

Create or participate in online forums and groups dedicated to your subject matter. Engage in discussions, share insights, and answer questions related to your textbook.

Collaborate with Educators

Collaborate with educators who adopt your textbook in their classrooms. Offer support, gather feedback, and showcase success stories from their experiences.

Partner with Institutions

Partner with educational institutions, bookstores, and libraries to increase the visibility and adoption of your textbook.

Summary

Marketing and promotion are integral to the success of your bestselling textbook. Crafting a well-thought-out marketing plan, leveraging digital platforms, engaging with your audience, and building a community of educators and learners are essential steps in reaching your target audience effectively. Embrace the opportunities of the digital age and use various promotional strategies to create a lasting impact in the educational landscape. By continuously engaging with your audience and fostering a sense of community, your textbook will become a trusted and sought-after resource in the field of education.

TECH
ADAPTION

In today's rapidly evolving digital landscape, embracing technological advances is crucial for the success and relevance of your bestselling textbook. In this chapter, we will explore the importance of adapting to digital formats, utilizing interactive content and online platforms, and addressing accessibility and inclusivity in your textbook.

Embracing Digital Formats

Traditional print textbooks are no longer the sole means of content delivery. Adapting to digital formats offers numerous advantages and widens the reach of your educational resource.

eBooks and e-Textbooks

Consider offering your textbook in eBook and e-Textbook formats. Digital versions allow for instant access, easy updates, and interactive features, enhancing the learning experience.

Interactive Multimedia Content

Integrate multimedia elements like videos, animations, and interactive simulations to reinforce concepts and engage learners more effectively.

Mobile Compatibility

Ensure that your textbook is mobile friendly and compatible with various devices. Mobile access allows learners to study on the go and provides greater flexibility in learning.

Utilizing Interactive Content and Online Platforms

Interactive content and online platforms offer new opportunities for enhancing the educational experience and fostering active learning.

Gamification

Incorporate gamified elements, such as quizzes, challenges, and badges, to make learning enjoyable and motivating for students.

Learning Management Systems

Collaborate with educators and institutions to integrate your textbook into popular

Learning Management Systems. LMS platforms offer seamless access to course materials, assessments, and progress tracking.

Open Educational Resources

Consider sharing parts of your textbook as Open Educational Resources, allowing educators and students to access specific chapters or sections for free. This can promote wider adoption and increase visibility.

Addressing Accessibility and Inclusivity

Ensuring that your textbook is accessible to all learners, including those with disabilities, is essential for fostering an inclusive learning environment.

Providing Alternative Formats

Offer alternative formats for learners with disabilities, such as audio versions for visually impaired students or transcriptions for those with hearing impairments.

Text-to-Speech and Readability

Design your content with readability in mind. Use plain language and ensure that the text is compatible with text-to-speech tools for learners who benefit from auditory learning.

Visual and Design Considerations

Ensure that images, graphs, and other visuals are accompanied by descriptive alt-text to aid learners with visual impairments. User Testing and Feedback Seek feedback from diverse learners, including those with disabilities, to identify potential accessibility barriers and make necessary improvements.

Summary

Adapting to technological advances is vital for staying relevant and effective in the ever-changing educational landscape. Embrace digital formats, utilize interactive content and online platforms, and prioritize accessibility and inclusivity to enhance the educational experience for all learners. By staying current with technological trends and continuously seeking ways to improve your textbook, you position yourself as a forward-thinking educator and author. Embracing innovation and inclusivity will ensure that your bestselling textbook remains a valuable and accessible resource for generations of learners to come.

QUALITY AND RELEVANCE

As an author of a bestselling textbook, maintaining the quality and relevance of your educational resource is paramount. Continuous improvement, responsiveness to changing needs, and staying up to-date with the latest developments in your subject matter are essential for the long-term success of your textbook. In this chapter, we will explore strategies to ensure the quality and relevance of your textbook over time.

Continuous Updates and Revisions

The educational landscape is constantly evolving, and your textbook should reflect the latest knowledge and advancements in your field.

Stay Informed

Keep yourself updated with the latest research, industry trends, and educational practices related to your subject matter. Attend conferences, read academic journals, and engage in professional development to stay informed.

Listen to Educators and Students

Encourage feedback from educators and students who use your textbook. Pay attention to their suggestions, comments, and critiques, and use this valuable input to make necessary updates and revisions.

Schedule Regular Reviews

Set a schedule for periodic reviews of your textbook's content. Consider revising and refreshing sections that may become outdated or obsolete.

Feedback Loop with Educators and Students

Fostering a feedback loop with your readership creates a collaborative approach to improving your textbook.

Surveys and Focus Groups

Conduct surveys and organize focus groups to gather feedback on the strengths and weaknesses of your textbook. Encourage open discussions on how to enhance the learning experience.

Online Platforms for Feedback

Leverage digital platforms, such as your website or social media channels, to solicit feedback from a broader audience.

Engage in Direct Communication

Respond to emails and inquiries from educators and students personally. Show that you value their opinions and are dedicated to improving your textbook.

Maintaining Academic Integrity

Academic integrity is paramount in educational publishing. Uphold rigorous standards to ensure the credibility of your textbook. Cite and Attribute Sources Provide proper citations and references for all borrowed content, including quotes, data, and images.

Avoid Plagiarism

Ensure that your textbook does not contain any plagiarized material. Use plagiarism detection tools to doublecheck your work.

Peer Review and Fact-Checking

Engage in peer review and factchecking processes to validate the accuracy of your content.

Adapting to Changing Needs

The educational landscape and the needs of learners are dynamic. Your textbook must adapt to these changing needs.

Address Emerging Topics

Include emerging topics and trends in your field that are relevant to educators and students.

Address Diverse Learning Styles

Consider incorporating content and activities that cater to various learning styles to make your textbook more inclusive.

Embrace New Pedagogical Approaches

Stay open to new pedagogical approaches and incorporate them into your textbook when appropriate.

Summary

Ensuring the quality and relevance of your bestselling textbook is a continuous journey. Stay committed to continuous updates, revisions, and feedback loops with educators and students. Embrace technological advances and changing educational needs to keep your textbook current and effective. By maintaining academic integrity and being responsive to the demands of your audience, your textbook will remain a trusted and valuable resource in the ever-evolving field of education. Your dedication to quality and relevance will leave a lasting impact on the learning experiences of countless students and educators who rely on your educational resource.

TIME MANAGEMENT

Writing a bestselling textbook is a significant undertaking that requires careful time management to ensure productivity and meet deadlines. Effectively managing your time during the writing process is essential for maintaining focus, avoiding burnout, and producing a high-quality educational resource. In this chapter, we will explore practical time management strategies and techniques to optimize your writing workflow and successfully complete your textbook.

Setting Realistic Goals and Deadlines

Establishing clear goals and is the foundation of effective time management for writing a textbook.

Break Down the Project

Divide the writing process into manageable tasks, such as outlining chapters, conducting research, and writing drafts. Assign realistic timeframes to each task.

Establish Milestones

Set milestones to track your progress throughout the writing journey. Celebrate each milestone achieved, as it will motivate you to continue.

Be Flexible

While it's crucial to have deadlines, be open to adjusting them if needed. Acknowledge that unforeseen challenges may arise during the writing process.

Create a Structured Writing

Schedule Consistency is key when it comes to writing a bestselling textbook. Establishing a structured writing schedule will help you stay on track.

Identify Your Most Productive Time

Determine when you are most alert and focused during the day. Schedule your writing sessions during these peak periods to maximize productivity.

Set Daily or Weekly Writing Goals

Assign specific word count targets or page goals for each writing session. Consistent progress, even in small increments, adds up over time.

Time Blocking

Allocate dedicated blocks of time on your calendar for writing. Minimize distractions during these periods to fully concentrate on your work.

Prioritize and Manage Distractions

Distractions can derail your writing progress. Learning to prioritize tasks and manage distractions is essential for efficient time management.

Use the Eisenhower Matrix

Prioritize tasks using the Eisenhower Matrix, classifying them as urgent and important, important but not urgent, urgent but not important, or neither urgent nor important.

Minimize Digital Distractions

During writing sessions, turn off unnecessary notifications and use website blockers to resist the temptation of social media or unrelated websites.

Set Boundaries

Inform family, friends, and colleagues about your writing schedule and request uninterrupted time during your designated writing periods.

Take Breaks and Practice

Self-Care Maintaining a balance between writing and self-care is vital for sustained productivity and well-being.

Implement the Pomodoro Technique

Consider using the Pomodoro Technique, which involves working for 25 minutes and then taking a 5-minute break. After four cycles, take a more extended break.

Engage in Physical Activity Incorporate

regular exercise or short walks during breaks to rejuvenate your mind and body.

Cultivate Hobbies and Interests

Engage in activities you enjoy outside of writing to reduce stress and maintain a healthy work life balance.

Summary

Time management is a critical aspect of writing a bestselling textbook. By setting realistic goals and deadlines, creating a structured writing schedule, and managing distractions effectively, you can optimize your productivity and achieve success in your writing journey. Remember to prioritize self-care, take regular breaks, and maintain a healthy work-life balance to sustain your creativity and focus. Embrace time management as a valuable tool to empower your writing process and create a transformative educational resource that resonates with educators and students alike.

CULTIVATING PATIENCE

Writing a bestselling textbook is a demanding and time-consuming endeavor that requires a considerable amount of patience. From the initial planning stages to the final publication, maintaining patience throughout the process is essential for staying motivated, overcoming challenges, and producing a remarkable educational resource. In this chapter, we will explore the importance of cultivating patience, how to navigate setbacks and delays, and the rewards that come with embracing patience in your writing journey.

Embracing the Writing Process

Writing a bestselling textbook is a journey with its ups and downs. Embrace the process and understand that it may take time to achieve your goals.

Accepting Iterative Progress

Acknowledge that writing a textbook involves multiple drafts, revisions, and improvements. Be patient with yourself as you refine your content to meet your vision.

Recognizing Small Wins

Celebrate the small achievements and milestones throughout your writing journey. Patience allows you to appreciate the progress you make, no matter how incremental.

Embracing Learning Opportunities

View challenges and setbacks as opportunities for growth and improvement. Patience enables you to learn from mistakes and continuously enhance your writing.

Navigating Setbacks and Delays

Unforeseen obstacles and delays are common in any large-scale project like writing a textbook. Patience is crucial for overcoming these challenges.

Adapting to Changing Circumstances

Stay flexible and adapt to unexpected changes, such as research challenges, personal commitments, or external factors beyond your control.

Managing Writer's Block

Writer's block is a natural part of the writing process. Be patient with yourself during periods of creative stagnation and seek inspiration from various sources.

Seeking Support and Encouragement

Lean on your support network, whether it's fellow authors, mentors, or friends and family, for encouragement and motivation during challenging times.

Practicing Mindfulness and Self-Compassion

Cultivating patience involves being kind to yourself and maintaining a mindful approach to the writing process.

Practicing Mindfulness Techniques

Incorporate mindfulness practices, such as meditation or deep breathing exercises, to stay present and focused during the writing process.

Practicing Self-Compassion

Treat yourself with compassion and understanding during moments of self-doubt or criticism. Recognize that writing a textbook is a significant undertaking, and it's okay to face challenges along the way.

Managing Expectations

Set realistic expectations for yourself and your writing journey. Avoid putting undue pressure on achieving instant success and focus on the gradual progress you make.

Savoring the Rewards

Writing a bestselling textbook is a rewarding experience that offers intrinsic and extrinsic benefits. Patience allows you to savor these rewards fully.

Celebrating the Final Product

When your textbook is published and reaches the hands of educators and students, take the time to appreciate the impact of your work.

Recognizing the Influence

Acknowledge the influence your educational resource has on the learning experiences of students and educators. Patience leads to a deeper sense of fulfilment from knowing that your efforts are making a difference.

Embracing Ongoing Impact

Embrace the lasting impact of your textbook on the field of education. Patience allows you to see the continued influence of your work long after its publication.

Summary

Cultivating patience is a fundamental aspect of writing a bestselling textbook. Embrace the writing process, navigate setbacks and delays with resilience, and practice mindfulness and self-compassion throughout your journey. By remaining patient, you can fully appreciate the rewards that come with producing a remarkable educational resource. The patience you develop will not only enhance your writing experience but also contribute to the lasting impact your textbook has on the educational community. Embrace patience as a valuable ally in your writing journey, and let it guide you toward the fulfilment of your vision and the creation of a bestselling textbook that leaves a lasting legacy.

MOTIVATION

Writing a bestselling textbook is a significant undertaking that requires dedication, perseverance, and unwavering motivation. While external factors can play a role in keeping you inspired, finding and harnessing your unique motivation is crucial for sustaining your writing journey. In this chapter, we will explore ways to discover your intrinsic motivation, overcome obstacles, and tap into your personal passions to fuel your creativity and drive while writing a bestselling textbook.

Identifying Your Intrinsic Drivers

Intrinsic motivation stems from personal interests, passions, and a genuine desire to create meaningful work.

Reflect on Your Purpose

Consider why you chose to write a textbook and the impact you hope to make in the educational landscape. Reconnect with your sense of purpose to fuel your motivation.

Identify Your Passions

Explore the subjects or topics within your textbook that ignite your passion and curiosity. Embrace these areas as sources of unique motivation.

Set Meaningful Goals

Establish specific, measurable, attainable, relevant, and time-bound (SMART) goals that align with your intrinsic drivers. Meaningful goals foster a deeper sense of motivation.

Embracing Your Personal Writing

Process Understanding your personal writing process allows you to tailor your approach to harness your unique motivation.

Identify Your Most Productive Environment

Discover the environments where you feel most inspired and focused. Whether it's a quiet study space or a bustling café, find the setting that enhances your motivation.

Embrace Your Writing Rhythm

Recognize your most productive times of the day and embrace your writing rhythm. Align your writing sessions with these periods to optimize creativity and productivity.

Embrace Your Writing Style

Don't be afraid to embrace your unique writing style and voice. Authenticity fosters a deeper connection to your work and amplifies your motivation.

Overcoming Obstacles and Challenges

In the writing process, challenges are inevitable. Your unique motivation will guide you through these obstacles.

Cultivate Resilience

Develop resilience to navigate setbacks and rejections. View challenges as opportunities to grow and improve your work.

Seek Inspiration

Seek inspiration from various sources, such as books, art, nature, or conversations with others. Inspiration can rekindle your unique motivation during difficult times.

Stay Committed to Your Vision

Maintain a strong connection to your vision for the textbook. Remind yourself of the impact your work can have on educators and students to stay committed to your writing journey.

Embracing Growth and Learning

Embrace a growth mindset and see the writing process as a journey of continuous learning and development.

Embrace Feedback

Value constructive feedback from editors, reviewers, and readers. See it as an opportunity to refine and enhance your work.

Learn from Challenges

View challenges and mistakes as learning experiences. Embracing a growth mindset allows you to see obstacles as stepping stones toward improvement.

Celebrate Your Progress

Acknowledge and celebrate your growth and progress throughout the writing process. Each milestone achieved is a testament to your dedication and unique motivation.

Summary

Discovering and harnessing your unique motivation is a vital aspect of writing a bestselling textbook. Aligning with your intrinsic drivers, embracing your personal writing process, and overcoming obstacles with resilience will keep you inspired and dedicated to your work. Embrace your passions, commit to your vision, and stay open to growth and learning. By tapping into your unique motivation, you will create a truly exceptional educational resource that reflects your passion and expertise. Let your motivation be the driving force behind your writing journey, leading you to create a bestselling textbook that leaves a lasting impact in the world of education.

www.ingramcontent.com/pod-product-compliance
Lightning Source LLC
Chambersburg PA
CBHW061001260726
48661CB00005B/1991